# ICELIGHT

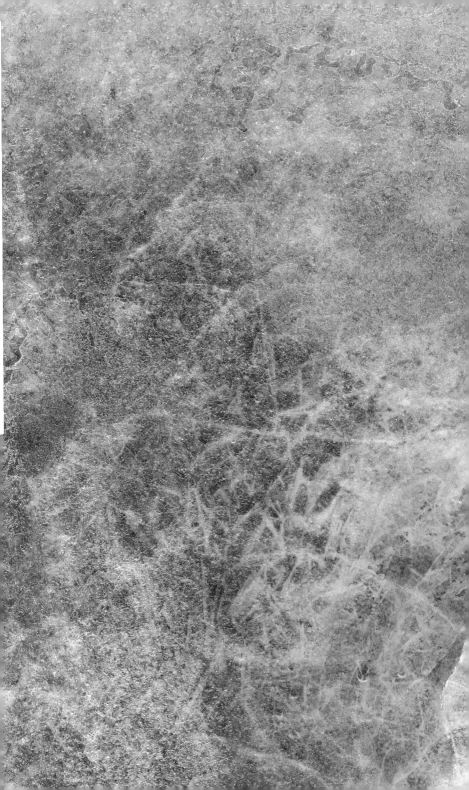

## Also by Ranjit Hoskote

POETRY

*Zones of Assault* (1991)
*The Cartographer's Apprentice* (with drawings by Laxman
   Shreshtha, 2000)
*The Sleepwalker's Archive* (2001)
*Vanishing Acts: New and Selected Poems 1985–2005* (2006)
*Central Time* (2014)
*Jonahwhale* (2018; in the UK as *The Atlas of Lost Beliefs*, 2020)
*Hunchprose* (2021)

POETRY (in translation)

*Die Ankunft der Vögel* (in German, 2006)
*Feldnotizen des Magiers* (in German, 2015)

POETRY (as editor)

*Reasons for Belonging: Fourteen Contemporary Indian Poets* (2002)
*Dom Moraes: Selected Poems* (2012)

TRANSLATION

*A Terrorist of the Spirit*, by Vasant A. Dahake (1992)
*I, Lalla: The Poems of Lal Děd* (2011)

ART CRITICISM

*Pilgrim, Exile, Sorcerer: The Painterly Evolution of Jehangir
   Sabavala* (1998)
*The Complicit Observer: Reflections on the Art of Sudhir
   Patwardhan* (2004)
*Zinny and Maidagan: Compartment / Das Abteil* (2010)

Wesleyan Poetry

# RANJIT
# HOSKOTE

*Wesleyan University Press   Middletown, Connecticut*

Wesleyan University Press
Middletown CT 06459
www.wesleyan.edu/wespress

Library of Congress Cataloging-in-Publication Data
*Names*: Hoskote, Ranjit, 1969– author.
*Title*: Icelight / Ranjit Hoskote.
*Description*: Middletown, Connecticut : Wesleyan University
    Press, [2023] | Series: Wesleyan poetry | Summary:
    "A collection of poems about transitions and departures,
    eloquent in their acceptance of transience" — Provided
    by publisher.
*Identifiers*: LCCN 2022038165 (print)
    LCCN 2022038166 (ebook)
    ISBN 9780819500533 (cloth)
    ISBN 9780819500557 (trade paperback)
    ISBN 9780819500540 (ebook)
*Subjects*: BISAC: POETRY / Asian / General |
    POETRY / Subjects & *Themes* / General | LCGFT: Poetry.
*Classification*: LCC PR9499.3.H674 I24 2023 (print) |
    LCC PR9499.3.H674 (ebook) |
DDC 821.92—DC23
LC record available at https://lccn.loc.gov/2022038165
LC ebook record available at https://lccn.loc.gov/2022038166

5   4   3   2   1

IN MEMORY OF *Raghuvir Narayan Hoskote* (1926–2021),

MY FATHER, MY FIRST GUIDE INTO THE LABYRINTH

You don't rise high in the celestial palaces—

at some point you go back down.

ANSELM KIEFER

# CONTENTS

## I

*Tacet*   *3*
Aubade   *4*
Retreat   *5*
Witness   *6*
Rock   *7*
*Noor*   *8*

Spur   *9*
Trigger   *10*
Groove   *11*
Fresco   *12*
Breath   *13*
Bed   *14*

## II

Eclipse   *17*
Night Ferry   *18*
Runner   *20*
Foreigner   *21*
Sentence   *22*
Wind   *23*

*Paishachi*   *25*
Apostle   *26*
Redacted   *27*
Postscript   *28*
Crow Hymn   *29*
What Did I Miss?   *30*

## III

All Gods Travel   *35*
Call If You're Lost   *36*
Plague   *38*
Juggler   *39*
The Mist Shop   *41*
Planet   *42*
Storefront Self-Portrait   *43*
Swimmer   *44*

Torso   *46*
Dust   *48*
Terminus   *49*
Bait   *50*

## IV

Icelight  *53*

Bookmark  *54*

Clock  *55*

Glover  *56*

Still Life with Oranges  *57*

Descant  *58*

Ocean Park  *59*

Slope  *60*

Tune  *61*

Exit  *62*

The Science of Detection  *63*

Miramar  *64*

## V

Column / *Vidisha*  *67*

Ritual  *68*

Temple  *69*

Matinée  *70*

Gravity  *71*

Talisman  *72*

In this Country of Silence  *73*

Monsoon Song  *74*

Title  *75*

Lesson  *76*

Anthem  *77*

Krishna's End  *78*

## VI

Catapult  *81*

Departures  *82*

Skeleton  *83*

Under the Southern
   Cross  *84*

Neighbours  *85*

Fleece  *87*

Mission  *88*

Afternoon Poem  *89*

The Harappan Merchant's
   Complaint  *90*

Switch  *91*

Roar  *92*

Return  *94*

Acknowledgments  *97*

Notes  *101*

I

# TACET

She stood under a drizzle of copper leaves
mouth opened in a hymn of praise
Voice *tacet*
Only the chirping of sparrows
heard on the terrace
above the sleeping town

Be opaque
her sisters had said
because this crust
is what will get you through
Standing above the chasm
opened in the eastern rock she thought

What if there was no border
between flesh and light
What if I had
no skin
Of what
am I the barometer?

## AUBADE

Rumours of wind, banners of cloud.
The low earth shakes but the storm
has not arrived. You pack

for the journey, look up, look through
the doors at trees shedding their leaves
too soon, a track on which silk shoes
would be wasted, a moon

still dangling above a boat.
Wearing your salt mask, you face
the mulberry shadows.
The valley into which
you're rappelling

is you.

# RETREAT

This floor is wet with the sea's retreat
        A draggled wing
drapes its shadow on the bell tower

Admiral, your telescope!
                Hold fast
The storm could have knuckled you to the floor

Voices wash through the sailor's sleep
        He scoops darkness
from darkness

The surveyor continues to look
           for a world at the other end
of his spyglass

knowing it's out there
        a distant cousin to the one
                that's blowing up around him

# WITNESS

Speak, Earth,
        in consolations of dewbud and darkening ray

turning to coal and slate in the cold mineshaft
        where I laid my hand

on cryptic passages carved from tidal night
      while voices hurried

through the locked air
        men with sharpened arrows

*Look for him!*
      I've found the seed bed, Earth, I wait for you

to say: It's time. Let me tell you
        why you're here

## ROCK

Now call it rock this edge
                          between your feet and blue

on a scarp thrust up from the seabed
                          *uma grande onda*

the nearest house a mile away
                  the nearest voices travelling

overhead through cables
                  tossed from pylon to pylon

Jump and you'll be one
                  with all there is to know

the missing piece of the puzzle
                  joining the Unknown

Its lava magnet heart still casting a field
                  through moss and bramble

the rock holds you in place

## NOOR

*i. m. Zarina Hashmi (1937–2020)*

Pinpricks of light
        in the sky's black yurt

Looking up from a rutted road
        as our clay-spattered boots

make common cause with shovels
        and burst tyres

our eyes narrow and widen
        to grasp the incoming code

But that light is both marrow and bone
        It defeats the gaze

*What we've lost*
        *reclaims us*

Who can translate
        its pulse?

## SPUR

Am I the boy
    who climbed this spur
and laid claim
    to the scrubland sweating
in its shade?

What coiled through me
    and sheared into space?
A memory of colours churning wet
        obsidian saffron jade
transmitted from other lives

*Have I stood here before?*

# TRIGGER

*i. m. Devapayya Nadkarni*

Let's assume
    I was that man with a bolt-action rifle
and a physician's split-handle bag
    heir to soldiers of fortune
       who left his copies of the *Modern Review*
to his daughters

who would remember that starling-loud evening
    he cradled his rifle and waited
on the back steps of his house
        for the last tiger in the Andlé forests
to prowl into his sights

*Man-eater, whose finger pulled that trigger?*

# GROOVE

Watch the earth contract
        to this groove in the blue rock
        from which water hurtles and air spins out
without curb or bridle

A groove that a twisted rod made
        when a prophet struck
        instead of speaking
as if the rock would not answer

He carried that groove
        unhealed
        to the last mountain he climbed
to kneel at the peak

clutching at that earth
        while his gaze plunged
        down steep slopes
to the promised land

## FRESCO


Why didn't they paint his face
    the same pale ivory they used for the faces
and his robes the same red ochre they used
      for the robes

of his companions?

He stands at the end of the row
    the seventh monk
a whispered outline
  at the bruised edge of the panel

dissolving into air

# BREATH

If that was breath I saw floating across the tracks
      without a single train to stop it
      while the parrots squawked in their fruited tree
I knew it would far out-distance the night

      spelling itself in one language after another along the route

leaving me to catch up
      halting and ranging in its wake
      calling out to it by every name
I have waited all my life to speak

# BED

A bed used to stand
                in that room of shimmering tides
Now a boat

rides at anchor there
         caulked
and ready to sail

through the mother-of-pearl shutters
We are
    what we've lost

# ECLIPSE

You waited all night for the eclipse.
A panther loped down to the lake
and swallowed the moon.

Another night you thought the wind
had called for truce. The moon
never crossed the laterite border.

A third night, searching in this field
where the sky had rained stars,
you found the moon

buried in a furrow that a yoked bull
had measured in loops from left
to right to left, turning

and returning. Speak, lunatic angel,
which was the right way?
Was I implement or impediment?

All night the eclipse waited for you.

# NIGHT FERRY

Try modest ambitions
    fisherman wading into cirrus waters
trawl the first faint stars of evening

It's too much work for the hunchback moon
    to take a shovel
to water that's gleaming in the dark

and when you find the horn-handled oar
    that fell out of the sun's barge one stormy day
fifty years ago

call out

...

What is he
    a phantom from a lost chorus
going down to the boats
    a prisoner of the words he spoke
yesterday?
       Down the night watches he goes
shouldering the canoe
       in which he splashed ashore

Waves advance
                    he shouts
           Don't trust the shore
Its ridges carry the heart's rivers
       that choked
                    when I gambled the ocean away
He throws himself
       on the riptide's mercy

Guide me where you will

# RUNNER

*for Steve Reich*

The rain never lies. It just shifts
the names of our seasons.

Deaf runner, it's time to outdistance your tribe.
Warm your compass on the ring of fire

in a fogged kitchen, write a history of the sky
as a steeplechase. Never be that man

with a diamond pressed into his forehead,
who gets on the S-Bahn

with a quiver full of arrows.
Or cycles into a broad river

without getting a good look
at the shore lights.

Lying among dead owls and cardinals,
he makes signals in shallow water.

*Save me*, he mouths as the tidemarks
dissolve, *from myself.*

# FOREIGNER

If you're a foreigner
>             language has not yet arrived
>             cycling through a field guide
>             every note spells a fretted shade
>             the door codes sound hoarse
>             monkeys speak Sanskrit
>             cotton in your ears doesn't help

If you're a foreigner
>             try carrying your own bugs
>             in transparent capsules
>             count till you hit sixty
>             wipe sweat only with silk
>             use soap only after midnight
>             the indigo road screams just once

If you're a foreigner
>             washrooms lead to firing squads
>             hands tied behind your back
>             you wake up to twin sirens
>             drink the wolf's despair
>             call out for the salt to subside
>             the results are at best ambiguous

# SENTENCE

This sentence of rushing water swirls
     around the silent hill where I first met snow
Let me take you by the hand she said
   let me show you where rock meets melt
how May's spasms get December's skulls
to break into flower and currents swell
     feeding the dry field where I fill
fossil fern with stolen sap
        This field is where
   I thaw into a thread and sew
these stacked pages of crystal and coal
    written over by scorch and snap
      these signatures that you turn
believing they were willed to you
       blank
waiting for your script to spell itself
     with detonator and backhoe

# WIND

At rainscatter twilight
    in a palace
past soldiers turned
        to stone chessmen

you led us up
        abandoned stairways
leading to galleries
           of thinnest air

In your breath
        I could hear the wind
tell tall tales
    of tying a gantry to a passing cloud

and clapping its hands
    as a thresher in a wheat field sang
songs of revolution
        in a year with no name

I sang sang the wind as long shadows broke
      and fell from their pedestals
leaving their feet
      trapped in marble

I sang the stories of all I'd lost
      when those marble shadows marched across
wide forests with fire and spade
      when they choked lakes

left them to clot and dry to salt
        knotted river currents
at tidemouth and blocked
         harbours with wrecked ships

No peace as I swept
        through this palace
at twilight
        no consolation

as our soldiers and theirs
    turned on each other
into each other
     in the rainscatter light
stone chessmen

## PAISHACHI

*i. m. Mohammad Subhan Bhagat (1927–1993)*

Who's there? I ask. Unknown hands have rifled through my notes.
Not me, says the lamplighter. I can't read the language of ghosts.

Pausing in their lullabies, the village women tell me no one's home.
They've gone to hunt or be hunted, wearing the iron shrouds of ghosts.

I could try and find them, who should fear them the most.
They whisper in foreign accents, trained in the tactics of ghosts.

Our grandfather sits alone. Around his fire, deer, bears, wolves
listen as he sings into the dark, doing the treble voices of ghosts.

They'll need more fur, more teeth, more claws to act on his boasts.
He calls up battle, flight and death, the circular memories of ghosts.

In gusts, bursts and torrents, Gunadhya's stories will flood the ocean.
He chants in a forgotten tongue, growling the vowels of ghosts.

His words sound like nothing that guests have ever spoken to hosts.
This is the language of my people, the language of living ghosts.

# APOSTLE

Clean your spear
apostle of silence
what legacy will you leave?

*Not the shadow the darkness*
*not the mask the face*

Why would I rise from my body?
What is that ruby-coloured fruit?

...

Guest from the future
gather the candidates
at the missing step

*Distance is the spur the tangent*
*streaking across the map*

Drought's the harvest not the cue
Every night in the cave I dreamt of lions

...

Chemist a thousand graveyards
could be accommodated
on your shelf

*Tell me what holds you up*
*what keeps you going*

I stand firm
because I stand nowhere

## REDACTED

This poem was not found in his manuscripts
not secreted in the labyrinth of his conversations
    not slipped into the transcripts of his published interviews
not heard on the bootleg recordings of his lectures
    not tucked into the dossier of photographs in his archive
not located on the hard drives he left behind
    not sorted among his xeroxes and index cards
not dispersed among the notes of his entourage
        Chased by prosecutors fanning their collars
flashing across banners wayward as the wind
    nothing conclusive you understand
this poem may never be found

# POSTSCRIPT

What if one day you scanned the sky and found
no trace of terns that, homing, crest the tide,
no arc of gulls gliding towards mirage shoals,
their journeys stalled, the winds too strong
or their wings not strong enough?
What if the earth slowed down, pulled off its gloves
and raised its knuckles to the late spring?
Would you defy the whiplash fates and craft
subtle compensations for the baffled will?
Would you try for balance as you climbed
the broken slopes of cloud, and shaking
between whisper and shout,
would you voice the poet's oldest fear:
What if one day the words refuse to come?

## CROW HYMN

*Krähe*
>  call out to the unknown god whose shrine
> is this sentence
> call him to feast on our ancestors
> who crossed the bridge into night

*kafkafkafka*
>>  this entrailed sentence
>> in what half-cindered words?

*Kagvā*
>  sing to us of the gold wings you sighted
> through the rain of ash
> sing to us of lovers taken away in chains
> to feed their sweat to jute and sugarcane

*kafkafkafka*
>>  this rain of cinders shards shrapnel
>> in what river-smoothed script?

*Kràhr*
>  bring us in whispers news from all corners of the world
> bring us in glass jars storms from all quarters of the mind
> bring us in treble chains the guardians of the forests
> we're about to torch with megaphones

*kafkafkafka*
>>  these storms in which you sing black-feathered hymns
>> in what scorched and strangled voice?

# WHAT DID I MISS?

Children of this sawdust town
play with the birds you've caged
    Watch them duel and dance
    in the marketplace
jabbing and pecking at one another's feathers
      like angry poets

*Tell me, what did I miss?*

The arch of spiders' webs
    the laughter of girls
going down to scoop
    the sun's heart from the water

*Or?*

A motorcade of clouds
   posing the coast a riddle
it could never solve
   the day's pink edge
caught in the sky's slant gaze
     the laughter of owls

*What did I really miss?*

The fathers are dark the mothers catch fire
    They've made promises they can't keep
The ocean is shuffling from one fluted skin
    to another
Most mornings I spear-fish for rainbows
perched on the broken sea gate
     that barely crests the tide

*Anything else?*

The lights wink on and off down the drowsy runway
What's missing at 5 a.m.
                           is the heart
of this star-shaped fruit I've sliced

*And?*

Expand
        You are not the panther
        the wardens hope to cage or tag
Contract

*Tell me again, what did I miss?*

I'm waiting at the breakwater for the big spinnaker to bloom
in the east
                coaxing the shaken cantilevered hills
to link together
in a final landscape

No flights land

*This was not going to be my story*

No one's immune
                You take your life
in your hands each time you cross
the street

*Was I missed?*

Alone each of us
      a syllable pulled from a checklist
or a blessing
   a dream a transcript or a curse

sentenced
      to fracture
how shall we
form words again?

## ALL GODS TRAVEL

*for Arundhathi Subramaniam*

All gods travel
    some ride camels
    others ride catastrophes

some shimmer along a pealing bell
      others chase tow trucks
      taking turns to ball their fists
      or stick their tongues out
      some hide in your sleeves
      or become spiders at nightfall

and some remember they were packed
      into camphor-scented chests
      carried across rivers
      bridging bloated days and shivering nights
      until they pressed down on the cart
      to call halt

*Here's ripe stone here's silvered creek*
      *here's the call of a flute*
      *trees praised in three tongues*
      *a harvest of shade*
      All gods travel
      but when we want them to stay

some turn their backs on us
      pat an aging dog on the head
      and look out to sea

# CALL IF YOU'RE LOST

*afterimages of Cartier-Bresson*

Rainbows are born
in broken windows

Go down that flight of stairs
Cross the street

into a century of shadows
and their squealing children

...

Double-check the water tower
that's timed to dissolve at noon

Wait for the alarm to ring out
the dry-tongued bell

...

Look back and enter them
in the ledgers of havoc

Men in turbans veiled women on mules
crossing swollen rivers
                    on pontoon bridges

charting detours
to throw pursuers off the scent

...

The dome slaps its shadow
against the whitewashed wall

It comes to rest on the head
of a man claimed by sleep
among crumbling bricks

In sleep's courtyard
a sentence chased by echoes
comes looking for a script

It crosses a kohl threshold
into the muezzin's eye

...

The *killari* bull might have gored
that horizon with its crescent horns
A mule limps into view
   Airtight peasants scour
the hoof-hard ground for roots

The foreground arrives late
panting
   the stagehands pick up
a grease mask tossed aside
by a mechanic in a hurry

Collect them in your notebook
   an orchard sown with charcoal
   a wisp of water tower
the gardener's last prayers
the drought's arrears

## PLAGUE

Those who ran to hide were stoned
     and chased from their fields
The juniper was fragrant the vinegar how strong
        but summer burned its way through the bricks
and the plague bell tolled

*Today we feast tomorrow we die*
     the drunks were neighing but no door opened
Every roof was heavy with crows
     Calling for a rain of fire the sturdier peasants sang
above the swaying crowd above its dense nose-lock of sweat

When their backs bent at last and their voices fell
     a monk cowled in fury
      whipped their song with a carrying drone
*Fields of sulphur to the right*
     *fields of scorpions to the left*

*Those flames scourges those flames sharp*
     *as flint twisted in our wounds*
River of souls surging to the hell he painted
     their bodies left nailed to the doors of heaven
     Ash-heaps the houses past which their song rose again

and no one to wipe the blood from every word

# JUGGLER

You need help
             standing at attention
knapsack on back
on wave-thumped turf
you've got this far
             At first light
undeciphered time
                you're ready to start

...

Take it as it comes
             juggler
Look in the spice-grinder's vat
Mind
      your tricorne head
Here comes the iron
               thump
Watch it jump

...

Spar with prime numbers
Enter the castle
            through a loophole
Climb
      to the top of the horsemen's tower
Listen to the light
rain on the terrace
              If tigers could cry

...

Time
    to call back your powers
Pounce
      on saint-blessed cambric
      rivers traded for silver
      dormant ammonite
Look out
      for what comes next

# THE MIST SHOP

In the lost and found department of the mist shop
   we scoured the stacks
for oil-slicked bay and casuarina stand
    Twisting around in this rodeo season
of mustang tides we breathed out and bumped
    into starched stretched ballooned ourselves
in a section advertising every shape and brand
   of mirror

We ducked veered tilted away from the earth's axis
    rose to cloud forests dove to sunk islands
in the television screens in the department next door
   *Take it as it comes* said the acrobat
who badly needed a haircut
     perched for the day among macaws and cockerels
at a counter across the aisle
    their eyes gleaming their beaks torqued

concave convex anamorphic as Holbein's skull
     ready to swallow
you and the street and the houses across the street and I
    could have sworn that was a comet
whooshing down the blocks or is that just
      a man in oversize silver overalls
scattering pomegranate seeds from a torn gunny sack
    on the sidewalks as he goes?

# PLANET

Don't read the world you're posing next to
      its script is dense and pictographic as Mars
Every planet rises
            and shakes you to the core
with its vaporous silver jalapeño tides
its thwarted channels and melting poles
      We're boats
      anchored in salt
or coasting along roads
          that illusionists are laying
across the bay
       as if the future were theirs
       to mine
About time
      this blunted earth opened up and swallowed
      its shiftless sons
      its reckless daughters
      its steeply tilted lighthouses

# STOREFRONT SELF-PORTRAIT

What I'd like from the sea
     is an assurance
that I could chronicle all my pirate pasts
    and go missing

between a rusty telephone booth sprayed with graffiti
      and a bulletin board patchworked
       with rival posters for the district elections
a shadow hurrying past a glass storefront

heavier at fifty than it was at twenty
      no longer a gymnast springing on the trampoline
just an anxious ghost filing his scrimshaw memories
      as he shuffles between roles

# SWIMMER

*for Vivan Sundaram*


Ploughing through dark waters the back a bare island

fallen from raft toppled from overloaded dhow shoved off
      sputtering launch
      scarred by sun salt propeller
           or lash of rigging come loose in a storm

*Indorsare*

To write on the back

with suture preserved
        as uncommon weal
    to seal with welt
           conclude with clot

...


This pitted skin is its own beach
        on which gulls take off and land

Where no one can sing in the dark
        this body is its own lighthouse

island quarantined
        from its archipelago

...

In the dim light
                four plaster casts
floating
          ghosts of sculpture
                          until decades later cast in bronze

# TORSO

Streetfighter and knife-*baaz*
        Caravaggio painted flesh with shrewd love
knew what it meant to slash at skin
        and spoil its alabaster finish
to thrust a dagger through folds of flesh
        aiming to carve the organs
throbbing beneath the sweaty membrane
        to savour the burst of blood
released into harbour air
        stinking of rotten fish

...

Caravaggio's apostle
        probing the risen Saviour's side
doubts the Resurrection
        but is also worried
about value in exchange as he weighs and gauges
the effect of the gash
        assesses the depth of the wound
calculates
        what probable reduction it might prompt
in the price

...

Whose torso
        broken by oxcart
        harrowed by knout
survives the canny butcher's appraisal?
A prisoner's
  dredged from a cistern?
A runaway slave's
  to be offered on the block again?
What belongs to a slave
        no price could cover it

# DUST

This golden light you see is all dust.

If you'd noticed that when you began to hunt
for the things that had escaped us
over stalled monsoons and cayenne summers:
                              Sparrows, missing from the corner
of your eye. Partridge clouds, trailing, lost at night.
Quadrants hanging, left unhinged by contrary winds.

And while our stars rusted, the planets
—born wanderers, frugal, nimble, stayed
one leap ahead, one hand-span out of reach.
How long before

we caught up or gave in?

Our trees grew sour and blanched as their mistimed fruit.
The sun's slightest breath would melt the ice
in our glasses.
                  Skimming from one
castaway island to the next on a brittle sea,
we trained our lenses
on skies that were trying hard
to tell us what the lions found out
when they met the gun.
That apex and base are just the same
and every predator ends as game.

The golden light that's left is all dust.

## TERMINUS

It must be you they're leaving behind
                single tracks laid in frosted ground
pointing in different directions
         Close to your heart you hold
a constellation of rusted stars

## BAIT

The only tree of tomorrow
rises above an orange sash
of sunset
pinned to the deck
of a drifting boat

The last fisherman

is wading into the river
every line cast
aside
as he splashes
towards a wave of ash

himself the bait

# IV

# ICELIGHT

Noctilucence
               blue icelight dripping
from a cloud

How to be the earth
             maimed and gloried
by that one stroke?

In a cave
           thawing in bearskins
by fireglow I carve

wings and a beak
            in flame-red stone
not hunting or hunted by

this one with a ridged mane
           and clawed arrows it will aim
to declare nightfall and daybreak

this one
          that I will buff
and never name

# BOOKMARK

*for Amma*

The world is everything that is the case. And was?
Would the world be everything that was three weeks,
seven months, a year ago, the case? You took
the sun with you, left behind just a dull shade
of bright, a trail of sloughed skin, a casing.
Let no one think the world is everything that is the case.

From sixty years ago, your notes in the margins
of your Keats: is that the case? Your hazel eyes
closed. The last thing you asked me:
*Do the parrots still nest*
*in the tree outside your window?*
A question I'll never hear again
but there's the tree, every leaf a flame, the parrots
flying around it in green garlands. Is that the case?

# CLOCK

*i. m. Raghuvir Narayan Hoskote*
*(1926–2021)*

When I open the door
to wind the clock
nine decades of starlings
fly out
      The key startles
the spotted deer rescued
from the railway tracks
      the mule stumbling
on the narrow mountain path
   I hear the river's chill crystal waters
rushing past the Sanskrit fears
of plainsmen
           the ocean washing
at the stone bridge
      that angry gods had once crossed
I hear plainsong rise to touch the clouds
      from Lighthouse Hill
and the face reflected
      in the pendulum
      as I steady and swing it
is my father's

# GLOVER

*for Sukhada Tatke*

She slips her trusting hands into a pair of leather shapes:
    her fingers slide through silk and settle in a grip
around her phone, a flask, a map,
        whatever talisman she raises
          against the cold.

Those kidskin hands encase, take the outline of her own:
    they learn the code of the digits, the span
of each phalange, what fragrance on which tips might tempt
  the opposable thumb, the kiss
        when lining meets knuckle.

Savage origins of those civil twins:
    stamped and sheared on an iron bed,
the hunt stitched into their seams, the cull
  smoothed into their palms, winter's wine mulled
in the vacuum around which their fingers twisted.

From passion's flayed hide the glover trims
    silhouettes of regret. She reaches out. Her gloves touch
his hands, which had once held everything
    and let it go.

# STILL LIFE WITH ORANGES

As boats shear past through the pearl-grey haze
our eyes widen to grasp a bowl of oranges.

The prism of this moment sacrifices more
than flesh, pips and rind at the hour's altar.

Each fruit bursts in variants of bright:
shine, glow, gleam and a tinge

of hope. To this bonfire we feed
our strained cages of skin and need

as we launch ourselves into the tide,
creatures crafted from cloud and night

given safe passage and brief voice
by the caprice of this shifting pearl-grey light.

# DESCANT

*for Nancy*

Be again

that girl in blue
walking down
the terraced steps
to the sunken garden

Descant floating high
above desert strings
breath of oranges
song free

from any words that might bind it

# OCEAN PARK

*i. m. Richard Diebenkorn (1922–1993)*

Call this landscape abstract if the world's splendour
meant nothing to you. If honking trailer trucks, steel sheets,
slate roofs in rain were just notations. If the sky could be sky
only if its dusty clouds were annunciations. If mottled teal,
rust, tan and lavish cobalt could come unhooked
from storefront and seaface, leaving nameless and bare
an ochre streak of hillside. Or boardwalk. Who cares?
That gaunt profile of terrace or deck
should have been a clean axis or plumb line.
And flag that jetty thrusting out to meet the tide
as an exercise, just that, for a brush tuning itself to Form.
You're translating as you take a slow, shambling walk
around a roomful of canvases: doors that slide
open and ask you politely to take a long fall through.

## SLOPE

Climb
    leaving nothing behind
    on this slope
    except the shrine
    you crafted from pebbles
    and lapsed pieties

I'll sit
    hunched under this mango tree
    drunk on water I've winched up
    from a moss-choked well

I'll wait here
        under so many moons
        my coat fraying my voice
        learning to hiss and roar
        my arms turning to sunstone

as I raise them to touch the wide silver-stranded cobweb of the sky

# TUNE

Do you know

what tune your body is humming
faint echo of call and response

as it prompts the reluctant arrow
on the weighing machine?

# EXIT

Choose
      your exit

Oxygen mask clamped
      to your face
      your switch toggled

Or as summer fades
      into monsoon rain
      hearing the flame whimper
      in a cistern of its own wax

Or after single-minded years
      of following your *Schwanz*
      running out and hugging
      a broken carthorse
      that a man was whipping
      to death in the street

Or on this serrated pepper leaf
      dipped in ginger paste
Taste it

# THE SCIENCE OF DETECTION

The man with cats' eyes can see in the dark
    shoeprints toppled chair glint of unsheathed kukri
He cannot see the dark

# MIRAMAR

*for Vivek Menezes*


Watch that shape
                as it stretches itself into moon,
                cloud, tunnel between worlds,
                trail of ash-blue leaves

Watch it chase
                the tail-ends of words
                drifting away from what they mean,
                birthing echoes that ask:

Will there be time
                for you to bridge
                these casuarina islands
                yawing on a tide of fireflies?

To turn your back
                on lighthouse and sea wall
                and be the foam
                on the crest

of the breaking wave?

## COLUMN / *Vidisha*

This column was crowned with an eagle the guide says
when this crossroads was a capital

The Greeks came here to pray
It stands in the unseasonal rain

on a pedestal of broken bricks
that can't fend off ferns and creepers

The girl hears behind her
the rattling tambourine

of a man leading a chained bear
that must dance for their meal

She turns to stare
at a column of chain-mailed horsemen marching south

## RITUAL

He sits alone in a room broader than a river
his song choked to a rivulet

The supple girls have bathed him in milk
fed him grapes and honey
and themselves

Tomorrow they will dance at the festival
as he burns

# TEMPLE

This road leads to the forgotten temple
    that hard-faced men towed here with straining hawsers
    a century maybe more ago

In the middle of the line you are writing about the temple
    you will forget the word for tiger and wait
    for the circus tent to go up and the flags of all nations

to flutter in an air so clear you could read
    newspapers by starlight
    but no headline could have seen ahead

how the circus hands would tear down the flags
    swarm to the temple and carry it off
    laying tracks to take it on tour

around the provinces uncaging among the crowds
    rushing to see the spectacle
    their forgotten and very hungry tiger

# MATINÉE

The old man sits on the black stone bench
wiping clouds and palm fronds from his glasses

He's waiting for the boy from the day-and-night pharmacy
to bring him his pills
                              Meanwhile the matinée he's replaying

is a movie in which a train charges hooting through a desert
a machine gun on its roof spraying bullets in all directions

spent cartridges clipping into the air faster than the eye
could follow and there's all of us there

who get in the way of that horizon-bound train
the Bedouin extras
                          wounded or killed by a script none of us wrote

# GRAVITY

To the man in striped pyjamas doing a headstand
on the pavement outside Phillips Antiques

everything falls up

A bronze cobra-crowned Shiva pointing south
shoots angry rays at him from the deep storefront

and a leather Hanuman dives into the clouds

Rest your wings a passing voice tells him
There's nothing above you nowhere to go

except an expanse of stone

# TALISMAN

Hiding behind the weekend
       you watch as the carpenter sizes up your boat
       and two old women start cutting your sails
       into nine coarse pairs of trousers

Take a break to look at the indigo clouds
       It's time you owned up
       to rinsing the heavens
       and hanging them out to dry

What do you think that huge fish was
       you hear the women whisper
       on which he rode around the whirlpool?
       He kept its skeleton by his bed his whole life

Here's where you crouch
       above these shimmering currents
       gripping a river stone in your paused hand
       powder-blue veined with white

A talisman
       the colour of home
       Throw it
       as far as it can go

# IN THIS COUNTRY OF SILENCE

In this country of silence
        soldiers are burning newspapers
missing hosts call to give their baffled guests
directions to the east harbour
which fills with the foghorns of unseen ships
        while plumbers hunt for silver spoons
        hoping their ladders won't give way

In this country of cunning
        patrons looking for doors in the wind
find that bats read floor plans better than architects
        What can I say about this magic show
        when across the shrivelling hours I see
the shops in the market bringing down their shutters
and the clouds apologise as a sandstorm rises?

In this country of exile
        charred wisps of newspapers float across the river
        no drumbeat follows no plucked string shivers
in their wake the sun is a searchlight
the jars in every stall brim with strawberry juice
and this tongue's gone dry
                        waiting for refugee songs to return

## MONSOON SONG

Days of grace, days of thunder.
Days when cold stone could have dreamt it was skin
born to carry the weight of saffron clouds.

Peace held us captive.
We who could speak were sworn to silence.
We who could sing were beaten like drums.

We ran, dodging havildar and thug.
We danced among nameless objects
in the garden of buried stories.

Our wrists ached, the choked sap rose
through our numb fingers.
Write all you know, the baobab said,

on these sheets of rain.

# TITLE

About that
>> wherever the turmeric bird
>> circles and lands

you'll find
>> a king who walks on stilts
>> his acrobats doing cartwheels

before him
>> his soldiers trotting behind him
>> his cooks bringing up the rear

weighed down
>> by griddles and cauldrons
>> his tailors struggling to keep up

with his strides
>> the robe they're trying to measure him for
>> stretching into a sovereign earth-coloured shroud

# LESSON

*for Asiya Zahoor*

The professor warned us not to say a word
He turned to the blackboard and drew a line

through our country with his screeching chalk
wrote two names to identify its broken parts

From today he said you can forget your flag
leave your spoken language at home

The wind rattled the classroom windows
He'd forgotten to chain it to the bent willow

The boatman on the lake outside was singing
The professor made a note to abolish him

We won't be needing these walnut screens he said
I'd like all of you to be completely transparent

When he clapped his hands and blew on them
clouds of chalk dust settled on our desks

burying them for years in snow

# ANTHEM

So much light
> against which a madman
> escaping the catacombs
> stalks butterflies

with a caltrop in his hands

He's just composed
> in stanzas put down
> during lucid intervals
> our anthem

a song of peace in the mouths of soldiers

## KRISHNA'S END

Gurgle of rising waters
                the tide is right cries of gulls
you thrash through sludge
                to stay in the dance
stay slay let go the blade
                take the arrowhead
aimed at your heel
        falter fall struggle to your feet
           in the forest of the gods
                as it sinks


vi rā ma
        the lock on your abugida tongue
breaks
      you find it in you to pause and praise
again
      the currents rush through and past you
stirring up white waves
        you pluck stories let go
           touch lives let go
hoot screech roar whisper ask forgiveness forgive


discover again every voice that spoke through you
        and now you lose your voice
your wound tells you
          what must be done
one last look back
        at the fading mangroves
beyond which the city you ruled
        till an hour ago is burning
you slip into the weighted canoe
                the tide is ripe

# VI

# CATAPULT

*for Joy Goswami*

Blindfold the boatman rows
       his sampan north along the creek
       the currents ripple in his wake
veined with green gravid with slick

Once out in the middle of the water he stops
       lets the waves buffet and torque his course
       as he throws coins
to twisting left and churning right

*Whatever it is it's coming for us*
       *hurling back all we hurled at it*

On the shore the boatman's twin
       has zipped on his spacesuit
       He's humming a zero-gravity tune
as he hoses every street and roundabout with bleach

Who can lasso the cyclone hurtling above their heads
       or corral the fever that's riding through town
       smearing huts towers shanties
with streaky red crosses

*Whatever this is*
       *who can breathe its name?*

# DEPARTURES

*for Ravi Agarwal*

What if the white mare dragged down by a flabby bridegroom
and underfed by her hungry syce

had the same name as the child ferrying bricks in her head pan
at the kiln?

What if the bat practising a dive behind the shuttered windows
of the Natural History section

could ask the elephant grazing in the parched scrubland
her name

which would not be one of the brightly painted names of the god
tucking his trunk in as his fans see him off at high tide

a departure viewed from the Towers of Silence by a tribe
of scrawny vultures contemplating their journey's end?

What if you tried to prise a password out of the stuffed orangutan
the taxidermists have enthroned as a totem at the zoo?

In all these names you'd recognise the lost and forgotten seeds
that a sleepy child dropped on the mossy ghats

as the pilgrims from the stars newly arrived swept past
one full-moon night in vermilion and brocade

Who could have told them they would meet us again
stripped of our gaudy masks our carrying voices muted

as skeletons on display
in a distant planet's Museum of Cautionary Tales?

# SKELETON

The last time I saw Eugenio Braganza's skeleton was when the movers were grappling with it on the stairs. They loaded it in the back of their truck, propping it up on a torn stuffed chair that had once been olive green. It tipped forward, settled over the broken baby grand, its bony hands preparing to play a sonata.

A workman yanked at the signboard that had advertised the nature of Eugenio's business and chucked it into the truck, narrowly missing the skeleton.

Up the seventeen mosaic steps. One look around, I thought, wouldn't hurt. The rosewood doors, carved with looped and knotted arabesques: yes, as solid as I'd always known them. But where were the velvet drapes, the phosphor outlines of the twin amphorae? And the redhead in the tutu, balancing her crown of swords? The sharks flying around the Gateway of India? The volcano that erupted during Cyclone Hengameh? Who had dared to fold up the night sky with its flickering Southern Cross? How to levitate with the kilim gone? Light boomed through the cat's-eyed darkness in which *THE GREAT GONZALO, Illusionist Extraordinaire*, had practised his arts for twenty-five years.

"*Chhe* men," came Eugenio's voice from higher up the staircase. "Party's over."

# UNDER THE SOUTHERN CROSS

You follow them
leaving the Big Dipper behind
chasing the Southern Cross

the woman who tied the winds in her bag
    the man who first struck fire from flint
the woman who first husked corn
    the man who tamed the horse
the twins who split their shadow in two
    playing warp against weft

Watch as they bend themselves a wheel
cast a bell
    truss up a ladder
    under the sky-nest spell out
an alphabet of hammer stirrup loom
   harrow sword dance

Again they break you again you craft
your tools
      burning
in the refiner's fire
always the apprentice
marking your transit
    with carbon roses

## NEIGHBOURS

His name is Chance
    baseball cap brim backward
flashy sneakers

he breaks in at your window
    remote in hand
ready to switch you off

or surf past to another channel
    and fill a plasma screen
with someone else's

screaming face.

...

Soldier-boy's made a pact with the stars
No one else can see them at noon

Move closer to the sky *Bogdan*
gift of God

He stares up hoping to collect a meteorite sample
in an empty beer bottle

His pants have fallen around his boots
his medals are pinned on awry

...

The man in blue overalls
tries to bribe Heaven with a book
that hasn't a hope in Hell

Backgammon for dummies?
The history of late 20th-century art?
Or just a petition for a safer world?

···

The woman in red overalls
lies mechanic-fashion
checking the suspension of a convertible
that's stalled in a slow-mo dream
the man in blue overalls
can't switch off and exit

···

The woman in the frilly pink housecoat
        has lost it big time
Curlers in hand
            she's running
She'll fall off the roof
        of the Tibetan restaurant
A Valium a baguette a momo
                the neighbours shout
Anything
            to guarantee her safe passage

All she'd wanted
        was a starring role
in her own biopic

## FLEECE

Word comes back
    from a border town
    trapped in an occupied country

The *wali* writes in code
    I'm sending you this fleece
    woven from mare's tail and mare's nest

It'll fit in your rucksack
    Fold it away with your sketch
    of the fragile midwinter sun

Hide them from the skinflint clouds
    until I can come back
    who's sent you nothing but warnings

Emcee of freak weather events
    I'll lift your tugboats in the desert
    They'll tow defunct countries behind them

as I chant spells from my Pashto grimoire and make it snow

# MISSION

I could have sworn there were two of me

one standing firm in gale-force winds, ear cocked for signals
the other slouching at his post, twiddling knobs on the short-wave

one watching the skies for drones or unmarked low-flying craft
the other turning the wet soil over, planting rows of seeds

one oiling his rocket launcher, plaiting concertina wire
the other watering his snake ferns and crotons

one waiting for a convoy of mud-spattered humvees to bail him out
the other back from tea in the village, hoping his orange trees will
fruit

# AFTERNOON POEM

Hour of quiet lanes and koels' cries
    when silk cotton trees burst in dead-end dreams
hour of houses with no latches or locks
    each wall a fluttering chronology of doves
hour when the home team's slogans spray-painted on a wall
    proclaim me a stranger newly arrived
hour of curved daggers with damascened blades
    aimed at my infidel heart

Unsung midway between aubade and nocturne

Hour that asks me to revise
    my trade routes
hour that divines
    my shortcuts and detours
hour that shakes my dusty afterlives
    from tasselled lampshades
hour that withholds
    my papers of departure

I pay this tribute to all the afternoons of my life

# THE HARAPPAN MERCHANT'S COMPLAINT

What do I care how these words sound
    in translation?
    *joppo—kshumpa— plaksha*

Make them count
    how many Maluku cloves
    how many carnelian beads

you can stuff into sacks
    bound by the shipload
    for Akkad

Make them measure
    stalls for the long-horned buffaloes
    we're trading west in droves

Make them weigh barley and wheat
    ivory and lapis lazuli
    not syllables for songs

Now decipher if you dare
    these words sealed in images
    the squat bull the sage lost in a trance

the horned man fighting a tiger
    Are these chants to cure the seasick
    or curses aimed at fleeing debtors?

Our fathers loaned us words we cannot spell

# SWITCH

Sixteen years to the night the hour
> the east windows frame the same moon
> that caresses the ageing terrazzo floors
> On the Kalamkari curtains
>> the hibiscus refuses to wilt

The exile steps into the dark room
> where he wrote his first books and reaches
> for the light switch
> touches flaking paint

wakes the cat and catches himself
> mid-passage in translation
> between nestling and rattled sea hawk
> tested by hurricanes

Should he have chalked a quick square around his feet
> waving off help?
> Voices brusque soft and ineluctably other
> crafted him a route out and back

Solo he would have bounced back to himself as drained echo
> Who would have heard him
> if he had cried out? What daimon lost
> between hostile languages
> carrying news from one battlefield to another?

## ROAR

Roar now or never
as we enter the garden of last lines

In this closing act
recall the shattered mountains

bend to the cough of a car engine
that should have purred

oil that rusty door hanging off its hinges
with a red velvet rag caught in it

nibble at the remembered plate of brown rice
sprinkled with crisp onion rings

outline the man saluting a flag
with a black cat perched on his other shoulder

Roar now or never
ask what is speech

that does not disguise its incendiary intent
does not betray the guileless traveller

does not carrot you with a better world
does not stick you with robot slogans

does not kill a zigzag with a homily
does not claim to save your soul

does not lay down the law on what comes next
does not embalm the hoisted dictator in song

does not capsize as it carries you across
the dividing river of fire

# RETURN

Open your eyes
to this rain that's here to stay

Centuries from now hurtling through space
this planet will host nightfog and dayhaze

on screens where once our lamplit faces
had flickered until they'd grown too hard to love

In the intervals when time reminds itself
how unbearable it is to keep calm and carry on

swelling the dark rivers that will churn and wash
through our ruined cities every staircase an Escher ghat

this rain

...

The far ship is a house marooned among scudding clouds
without captain or crew or faintest hope of landfall

All horizons hostile all compass points lost
a seagull losing height over snowy peaks

you call out in a world muted by mist
so mortal that the autumn trees

would cloak you in their final leaves
as you stumble towards the latched gate

out-of-breath traveller
stammering a word of thanks

light returns to the world

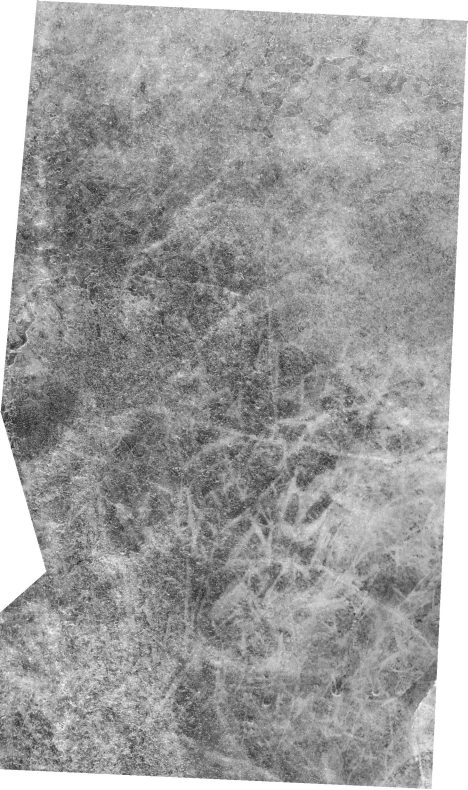

# ACKNOWLEDGMENTS

*I would like to thank the editors of the journals and anthologies where some of these poems were first published:*

"Aubade," "Breath," and "Bed" appeared in *Singing in the Dark: A Global Anthology of Poetry under Lockdown*, edited by K. Satchidanandan and Nishi Chawla (New Delhi: Penguin/Vintage, 2020).

"Retreat," "Witness," "Rock," and "Spur" appeared in *Poetry Wales* 56.2 (Winter 2020), edited by Jonathan Edwards.

"*Tacet*" was published in *Volume*, issue 3 (December 2020), edited by Madeline Gilmore and Daniel Hardisty; special thanks to Rebecca Levi and Lauren Peat on the editorial board.

"Groove," "Fresco," and "Eclipse" were published in *The Punch Magazine: Poetry Special* (February 2021), edited by Shireen Quadri.

"Plague," "The Mist Shop," and "Juggler" were published in *Divining Dante*, edited by Paul Munden, Nessa O'Mahony, Paul Hetherington, Alvin Pang, David Fenza, Moira Egan, and Priya Sarukkai Chabria (Canberra: Recent Work Press, 2021).

"Crow Hymn" was commissioned for the *Droste-Landschaft: Lyrikweg* project (2021), initiated by the Burg Hülshoff Centre for Literature / Annette von Droste zu Hülshoff-Stiftung, Münster, Germany.

"Apostle," "In this Country of Silence," "Fleece," "Ritual," "Talisman," and "Temple" appeared in *Conjunctions* 77 / *States of Play* (Fall 2021), edited by Bradford Morrow.

"Call If You're Lost," "Matinée," "Monsoon Song," "Skeleton," "Storefront Self-Portrait," and "Swimmer" appeared in *The Beltway Poetry Quarterly* 22, no. 4 / *Rooted* (November 2021), edited by Indran Amirthanayagam.

"Departures" was written as part of my contribution to the collaborative project *Samtal Jameen Samtal Jameer / Equal Terrains, Equal Beings*, conceptualised by Ravi Agarwal. It has appeared in *Mascara Literary Review* no. 27 / *Transitions* (December 2021), edited by Anthea Yang and Michelle Cahill.

"Ocean Park" appeared in *Plume Poetry* no. 126 (February 2022), edited by Daniel Lawless.

"Clock," "Miramar," "Gravity," and "Title" appeared in *The Green Integer Review*, no. 11 (January–February 2022), edited by Douglas Messerli.

"All Gods Travel," "Bookmark," "*Noor*," "Runner," and "Trigger" appeared in *The Best Asian Poetry 2021*, edited by Sudeep Sen (Singapore: Kitaab, 2022).

"Sentence," "Eclipse," "*Paishachi*," and "Monsoon Song" appeared in *CONVERSE: Contemporary English Poetry by Indians*, edited by Sudeep Sen (London: Pippa Rann, 2022).

"Lesson," "Switch," "Roar," and "Afternoon Poem" appeared in *The Bombay Literary Magazine* issue 51 (April 2022), editor-in-chief Anil Menon, poetry editor Pervin Saket.

*

*My very special thanks to:*

Suzanna Tamminen, director and editor-in-chief at Wesleyan University Press, who welcomed this book warmly, championed it, and piloted it through the review process.

Jim Schley, who brought a poet's sensitivity and sympathy to the copyediting of this book; I shall always cherish his fine discernment.

My agent, Priya Doraswamy of Lotus Lane Literary, for her tireless and enthusiastic support of my work, and her superbly revitalising transoceanic conversations.

My friend and delightful co-conspirator across domains, Sukhada Tatke, who read the manuscript that became *Icelight*, for her sensitive responses and astute insights.

Ruth Padel, for the blessing of her friendship, and the inspiration of her practice—which have seen me through seasons both dark and bright.

Forrest Gander, for his vibrant generosity of spirit, and for an illuminating dialogue on our planetary future while I was writing this book.

Douglas Messerli, for his world-encompassing curiosity about the literary, visual, and performing arts, and for his splendid collegiality over two decades.

Bradford Morrow, for a delightfully stimulating and generative exchange around a group of poems that appear here.

*And as always, I thank my wife Nancy Adajania for more than I could hope to put in words: for her love and patience; her sage counsel and wry humour; and for our journey together in life, literature, and the visual arts, which now spans more than three decades.*

The epigraph to this book is a quotation from *Anselm Kiefer: In Conversation with Klaus Dermutz*, translated by Tess Lewis (Calcutta/ London/New York: Seagull, 2019), 194.

## *"Paishachi"*

This poem takes its title from a nineteenth-century linguistic chimera that finds a tragic metaphorical resonance today. George Grierson (1851–1941), the founding Superintendent of the Linguistic Survey of India, advanced the claim that the Kashmiri language was descended from a fifth-century CE successor language to Sanskrit called *Paishachi*—literally, "the language of ghosts." Appropriately enough, no text in *Paishachi* is extant today, and the only work believed to have been composed in it is an *Ur* collection of stories attributed to the sixth-century author Gunadhya. Sheldon Pollock summarises the current scholarly view on the subject pithily: *"Paishachi* is the joker in the deck of South Asian discourses on language, having an exclusively legendary status, since it is associated with a single lost text, the *Brihat-katha* (The Great Tale), which seems to have existed less as an actual text than as a conceptual category signifying the *Volksgeist*, the Great Repository of Folk Narratives . . ." See Pollock's magisterial *The Language of the Gods in the World of Men: Sanskrit, Culture and Power in Premodern India* (Berkeley: University of California Press, 2006), 92.

While Grierson's theory about the origin of Kashmiri has been discarded, a "language of ghosts" asserts a claim over this poem, which takes as its setting the decades-long unrest in Kashmir: a situation compounded from insurgency, low-intensity warfare, civil strife, and the Indian State's military repression of local demands for autonomy. The worst excesses of this unrest took place in the early 1990s; among the many victims of the pervasive violence, at once physical and psychological, was the playwright, director, and actor Moham-mad Subhan Bhagat (1927–1993).

Bhagat had rescued the Valley of Kashmir's robust, satirical, and politically courageous form of folk theatre, the *Bhand Pather* of Akin-gom, from extinction. Unfortunately, he was destined to be one of its last great exponents. Torn apart by terrorism and State repression, Kashmir came under the sway of a militant brand of Wahhabi Islam, contemptuous of the Valley's organically rooted, gentle, and syncretic form of Islam—and rigidly opposed to music, theatre, cinema, and the arts. Wahhabi militants bombed cinema halls, humiliated musicians and broke their instruments in public, and confined Bhagat to his home. Silenced by forces inimical to the free, irreverent expression of ideas and opinions, Bhagat's voice became the voice of a ghost, of a society reduced to spectral cries and whispers.

## "Apostle"

### *"Guest from the future"*

The great Russian poet Anna Akhmatova (1889–1966), long isolated in the Stalin-era Soviet Union, described the philosopher and histo-rian of ideas Isaiah Berlin (1909–1997) as a "guest from the future" when he visited her in Leningrad (the once and future St. Petersburg) in 1945. To Akhmatova, the Latvian-born Berlin—whose prosperous and liberal Jewish family had migrated from Bolshevik Russia to the UK in 1921—represented a link to her vanished youth, and to a world of ideas beyond the giant gulag that the Soviet Union had become. To Berlin, Akhmatova embodied the ideals of beauty and stoic grace; he saw her as the heroic voice and conscience of poetry, resilient in the face of adversity and oppression.

This meeting had fateful consequences. Since Berlin was working with the British Foreign Office at the time, Stalin and his circle re-garded him as a spy; by meeting him, Akhmatova laid herself open to the charge of treason. She suffered brutal persecution in consequence; her son, Lev Gumilev, was sentenced to a decade of incarceration in a Siberian prison camp. Yet Akhmatova never lost sight of the hope of freedom and fearless expression that her meeting with Berlin had, however briefly, held out. See Isaiah Berlin, "Anna Akhmatova: A Memoir," in *The Complete Poems of Anna Akhmatova*, edited by Roberta Reeder, translated by Judith Hemschemeyer (Brookline, MA: Zephyr Press, 1997), 35–55.

*"Every night in the cave I dreamt of lions"*

This line is adapted from the account of one of the individuals interviewed in *Cave of Forgotten Dreams* (2010), Werner Herzog's 3-D documentary on the Chauvet and Hohle Fels caves, sites rich in art and artefacts from the Upper Palaeolithic era: "Every night I dreamt of lions."

The documentary may be viewed here: https://watchdocument aries.com/cave-of-forgotten-dreams/ (retrieved 6 May 2022).

*Chemist a thousand graveyards*
*could be accommodated*
*on your shelf*

These lines are animated by a macabre reflection of the avant-garde Polish-Ukrainian artist Kazimir Malevich (1879–1935): "In burning a corpse we obtain one gram of powder; accordingly, thousands of graveyards could be accommodated on a single chemist's shelf." See his "On the Museum" (1919), in Malevich, *Essays on Art 1915–1933*, Vol. 1, edited by Troels Andersen, translated by Xenia Glowacki-Prus and Arnold McMillin (London: Rapp & Whiting, 1971), 70.

# "Plague"

This poem incorporates some lines re-crafted from Jens Peter Jacobsen, "The Plague in Bergamo," translated by Will Stone, which appeared in *The London Magazine*: *Untitled, 2020* (special edition, 2020), 15–22.

## "Glover"

This poem was triggered off by an account of the Strazzeri family, who continue to make kidskin gloves in the traditional manner in Grenoble, France. See Sukhada Tatke, "The Delicate Art of Glove-making Lives on in the French Alps" in *Atlas Obscura* (21 January 2020). www.atlasobscura.com/articles/tradition-glovemaking-france (retrieved 6 May 2022).

## "Column"

The Heliodorus Column in Besnagar (Central India) is an *axis mundi*, dedicated to the deity Vasudeva in 113 BCE by Heliodorus, an ambassador to the kingdom of Vidisha from the Indo-Greek court of Antialcidas in Taxila (in present-day Pakistan). Heliodorus's inscription, composed in the regional Prakrit and set into the base of the stone pillar, constitutes the earliest evidence for the cult of Vasudeva, which would later be absorbed into the pan-Indian worship of Vishnu or Krishna, the Supreme Deity. It is a tribute to South Asia's capacity for transcultural confluence that the first self-avowed worshipper of Vasudeva in the historical record should have been of Greek descent.

Over the centuries, the column slipped into the realm of folk ritual practices. By the late nineteenth-century, it had come to be worshipped by the local community as a tutelary deity, "Kham Baba," its inscriptions thickly encrusted with vermilion, its sculptural details overlaid with offerings. It was encountered in this form in 1877 by the archaeologist Alexander Cunningham; although broken and weathered, it was restored to some semblance of its original shape and purpose over the next four decades by the Archaeological Survey of India.

## "Lesson"

In August 2019, the Government of India took the unprecedented and draconian step of splitting the state of Jammu and Kashmir in two and demoting its newly created halves to the status of "Union territories"—areas controlled directly by New Delhi, without the participation of local political parties, in a manner uncomfortably reminiscent of colonial rule.

This step may accurately be interpreted as yet another gesture of repression in a long sequence of missteps, given Kashmir's vexed relationship with India—beginning with the former kingdom's absorption into the newly independent nation-state in October 1947—and the civil and military conflict that has prevailed there since the late 1980s, which successive administrations in New Delhi have refused to address through the modes of dialogue, conciliation, and healing.

## "Neighbours"

This poem was inspired by my experience of a multi-site work by the Moscow-born artist Anton Litvin, installed across a number of public sites during Manifesta 4 (May–August 2002 in Frankfurt-am-Main, Germany).

## "The Harappan Merchant's Complaint"

Two of the three words that appear in line 3 of this poem appear in the *Rig Veda*, the earliest collection of visionary poems, invocations, and hymns produced by the Sanskrit-speaking Aryans who entered South Asia from the steppes in several waves between 2500 and 2000 BCE. These words—*kshumpa* (mushroom) and *plaksha* (fig tree)— are not of Indo-European origin. Some scholars have suggested that they are loan words from the language of the Indus Valley Civilisation (IVC), a Bronze Age culture that the Aryans overthrew; the IVC's great urban centres, assaulted by the Aryans, are known to us only by the names of the modern archaeological sites that mark their locations: Harappa and Mohenjo Daro, formerly in British India and now in Pakistan. The third word, *joppo* (water), appears in Nihali, an endangered Central Indian language thought to be descended from the Harappan languages.

While we may guess at the survival of stray Harappan words in mainstream sacred literature and the vocabularies of marginalised communities, the Harappan script has resisted decipherment, despite the prodigious efforts of several generations of scholars since the 1920s. See Michael Witzel, "The Languages of Harappa": http://crossasia-repository.ub.uni-heidelberg.de/120/1/Languages Harappa_1998.pdf (retrieved 6 May 2022).

The IVC had strong mercantile relations with the Akkadian Empire in Mesopotamia: Harappan seals were discovered at the Akkadian sites of Ur, Babylon, and Kish before the existence of the IVC was known. In one of his inscriptions, Sargon of Akkad (2334–2284 BCE) refers to trade with "Meluhha," the name by which the Akkadians knew the IVC. See Daniel T. Potts, *Mesopotamian Civilization: The Material Foundations* (Ithaca: Cornell University Press, 1997), 134–35.

# ABOUT THE AUTHOR

Ranjit Hoskote is an Indian poet, art critic, cultural theorist, and independent curator. He is the author of more than twenty-five books, ranging through poetry, art criticism, cultural history, and poetry in translation. His collections of poetry include *Hunchprose* (Penguin/Hamish Hamilton, 2021), *Jonahwhale* (Penguin/Hamish Hamilton, 2018), *Central Time* (Penguin/Viking, 2014), *Vanishing Acts: New and Selected Poems 1985–2005* (Penguin, 2006) and, in German translation, *Die Ankunft der Vögel* (Carl Hanser Verlag, 2006). His translation of the fourteenth-century Kashmiri mystic Lal Ded has been published as *I, Lalla: The Poems of Lal Ded* (Penguin Classics, 2011). He is the editor of *Dom Moraes: Selected Poems* (Penguin Modern Classics, 2012), the first annotated critical edition of a major Anglophone Indian poet's work. As a curator of contemporary art, he has organized more than forty exhibitions since 1993. He co-curated, with Okwui Enwezor and Hyunjin Kim, the 2008 Gwangju Biennale in Korea; he was also the curator of India's first-ever national pavilion at the 2011 Venice Biennale, titled *Everyone Agrees: It's About to Explode*.